Shadows From the Cross

The last words of Jesus

Sylvia Casberg

Copyright©2013 by Sylvia Casberg

Sunny Fields Publishing
2162 Creekside Drive, Solvang, CA 93463-2239

Book design by Sylvia Casberg

First edition

ISBN   978-0-9827781-5-9

Dedication

To those who wait passionately for the empty tomb

and the scent of lilies.

Other books by Sylvia Casberg

A Christmas Passing

Praying the Seasons

A Time to Ponder

Shadows from the Cross

(The New Revised Standard Version of the Bible)

The First Word

"Father forgive them, for they do not know what they are doing." Luke 23:34a

page 7

The Second Word

"Truly I tell you, today you will be with me in Paradise."

Luke 23:43

page 15

The Third Word

"Woman, here is your son." Then he said to the disciple,

"Here is your mother."

John 19:25-27

Page 21

The First Word

"Father, forgive them, for they do not know what they are doing."

Luke 23:34a

Evil begets ignorance.   With great skill evil divests its offspring of memory.   From the garden of creation, no whispers of "good... very, very good," remain, no echoes of wisdom abide, only a witless inability to discern right from wrong.

Ignorance becomes an easy foil in the hands of evil, and these offspring go about their father's business impregnating the earth again and again with more depravity. From generation to generation the seeds of wrongdoing are passed until no one knows wrong is wrong. It is normal.

These normal people gather to crucify Jesus. They are not monsters. They are ordinary folks, curious about the order of the day. Some doing their duty, others making sure they do.

By the time a criminal gets to this hill, it is only a matter of waiting. This place of the skull is not for small-time convicts. Crucifixion is reserved for the big ones. And since Roman law provides the best system of justice in the civilized world, those who frequent crucifixions have no doubt these deaths are deserved. They are guilty.

Roman soldiers assigned to duty on Golgotha know the ropes. Some with a taste for torture get a high from blood and guts, separating this assignment from their lives at home. Some say they are better husbands and fathers after exorcising the brutal side of their personality at work. Others get sick, close their eyes, hold their ears, cover their nose and ask for a transfer, but not in time.

Another condemned one comes, dragging his cross beam toward the mound. He falls. A bystander is boxed into service by the guards, and on they strain.

Watching, the soldiers have no way of knowing this man is different. Some may have heard about his audience before Pilate, the Governor of Judea, who washed his hands in a basin of water, cleansing himself of responsibility, and passing on the hard decisions from one person to another, from one level of government to another, one roll of red tape rolls into another until no one quite remembers where it all started.

Spread the burden of guilt around. The more people involved, the more difficult to pin down any one person to hold responsible. Let the system hide the guilty.

"Father, forgive them; for they do not know what they are doing."

Few know of Judas' suicide. Betting his thirty silver pieces to call Jesus' hand: he lost. Still he hangs, food for carrion creatures, soon he will be picked to the bone. Dry bones of despair. A man known, but unknown, forever a question marking history.

"Father, forgive them; for they do not know what they are doing."

Consider those carpenters commissioned by the state to make crosses. The work is steady, and the pay is a pleasant supplement to their regular wages. Moonlighting, making use of lumber found at bargain prices, delivering in the shadows. Justifying their handiwork, "If I don't make it; someone else will. I don't use it. I just make it."

"Father, forgive them; for they do not know what they are doing."

The religious leaders, they aren't all bad. Not all know what they are doing, what the impact of their kangaroo court will be. Publicly, they are the last to admit wrongdoing. Secretly, they confess there were questions they couldn't answer, pressures to vote a certain way, factions they owed support. Politics, you know. You can't get away from politics.

Even more secretly, hidden in the darkest corners of their being, some know they had sold their souls.

This "Jesus problem" wouldn't go away, reminding them of prophets past, pecking away at the incumbent religious system in bygone days. Someone always raises up to rock the boat when everything is going smoothly. This Jesus is just another crowd rouser.

For a while, he added a little spice, a little diversion from the same old administrative problems within a religious institution, something to talk about over lunch.

But he went too far attacking the system. Time to put an end to him. After he is dead and gone, some of his ideas might be worth debating in a proper forum, but for today, he is just another minor prophet problem.

"Father, forgive them; for they do not know what they are doing."

Some know. Some know exactly what they are doing. False witnesses know, hired for yet another job of perjury. The end justifies the means. Important people told them to lie, if anyone is responsible, it is they. The pay is good. Center stage provides a chance to act, be applauded, and be respected by the religious system. A day in court is fun now and then. It's a job and it gets easier with each cross-examination.

"Father, forgive them."

The cumulative effect of all ignorance converges at Calvary. Sin has its day at the place of the skull. Evil crucifies the Christ of God while he prays for us.

Like carpenters building instruments of death, we close our eyes to the questionable work of our hands. Rationalizing dirty work, under-the-table work, deeds of darkness and expediency, we too need forgiveness.

Like Roman soldiers following orders and keeping the peace, sometimes we don't know wrong when we see it. We justify our deeds, letting ignorance masquerade as knowledge and set the stage for tragedy.

Peace at any price. Hearing no screams in the streets, we equate silence with peace. Yet, silence at the cost of justice cries out from within the soul, "Peace, peace and there is no peace!"

Like religious leaders studying scripture and debating the Torah, we quote the Bible to support our positions. How clever we are, dividing the church over dogma, dissecting the body of Christ to suit our parochial views, and scoring points in morality debates that may win arguments but lose souls.

Father, forgive us for those things we do in ignorance, in apathy, in haste and in self interest. Forgive us for those things we have left undone, washing our hands of responsibility rather than getting dirt under our nails. Forgive us when we stand silently at the edge of a crowd rather than following the man who strips down, takes towel and basin, then kneels to wash the feet of his friends.

"Father, forgive them, for they do not know what they are doing."

The Second Word

Truly I tell you, today you will be with me in Paradise."

Luke 23:43

Living east of Eden these many generations, all live just east of Paradise, just east of the garden where thievery all began. Today, a thief returns. The crucified one leads the way home this very day. Christ, the second Adam, opens the gates that closed to the first Adam long, long ago.

This one, God's new creation, was born among the beasts, lived among sinners, and now dies between thieves. This one pays the ultimate price to lead us home again, to Paradise.

He was born among the beasts, as his lowing, chewing, restless stable mates looked on. They too shared their beginnings in Paradise. Here it was they first heard their names, spoken by the first Adam. Here they knew peace in the company of all that moved and breathed and had its being. Predator had no meaning. Beauty reigned and order abounded. God looked upon Paradise, and it was good, very good.

Lived among sinners, he did indeed. They were his friends. He ate and drank with those who cheated at collecting taxes. He chatted comfortably with prostitutes, touched the untouchables and challenged demons. He, who knew no sin, knew sinners intimately, loved them, encouraged their childlike honesty, their humility, and their ready confession. They were the first to admit they didn't deserve Paradise.

Others who confessed no sin, who publicly professed their goodness, who pointed fingers at others and advertised their own generosity, these became his stiff-necked adversaries, too self righteous for the likes of him, too holy to stoop, too pure to bend. These were the greater sinners, living above the law they enforced, boasting they were due a birthright in Paradise.

He will die between thieves. One derides him saying, "Are you not the Messiah? Save yourself and us!" But the other rebukes these words, "Do you not fear God, since you are under the same sentence of condemnation? Our sentence is just. We are getting what we deserve for the deeds we have done, but this man has done nothing wrong."

Then he cries, "Jesus, remember me when you come into your kingdom." A simple plea, not to be denied.

"Truly I tell you, today you will be with me in Paradise."

Paradise is waiting for the penitent, the humble, the travel-weary wanderers, those who believe they can't go home again. But, they can.

It will be different from the home imagined. This home welcomes sinners, those missing the mark set for their lives, broken by the furies of desire, frustrated by interrupted dreams. These sinners know they need a guide. These strangers to Paradise can't find Eden alone. They are lost from Paradise.

Those who hang around crosses, watching those who hang upon them, wonder about tomorrow. As they wait upon the death of others, they worry about their own families and friends, their jobs and debts. They live as though there were no tomorrow.

But there is. For them life may be hard, but they want more days, more years, more decades. Death surrounds them and they are glad it is not their own. Tomorrow may hold troubles and sorrows, but they want to waken again with the sunrise, taste bread and fruit, see their friends, and laugh over a drink. They have time to wait on Paradise.

Those who hang upon these crosses have no tomorrow. A last sky fades over their heads. A final gaze at the city walls. Human voices fade into the chasms of torture. The smells of blood and urine mix with the taste of sweat. Lips salty, parched, cracking. Death breathes upon them, surrounds them, fills them, defines them. This is it, their last day on earth. Where will they be tomorrow?

Strange irony in the scheme of God, a thief is the first to come home, returning to the garden where stealing began. Yet perhaps not so strange in the cycle of God's comings and goings.

Adam and Eve stole forbidden fruit and were banished to slave labor with the work of his hands, and birthing labor with the pain of her belly. Banished from Paradise with stolen goods, fruit not so tasty now, bitter with disobedience, and the knowledge of good and evil.

Now the Crucified One makes a promise. He will return, and with him a thief. Punishment has come full circle one might say. Two left the garden, two are coming home. There could have been three, for three hung together in the community of the condemned.

One chooses life, and the other loses Paradise. One takes his due for the crimes he committed. The other dies cursing a system he tried to outsmart. Today is the day to decide. There is no tomorrow.

And so it is, one criminal is promised an eleventh-hour reprieve. Not for this world, but for the next. That's where it counts for eternity. In Paradise.

From a distance, bystanders wonder about Paradise. Does it have a geography, a history, a time, or is it a place of metaphor, of spiritual reality, of truth beyond actuality?

Is Paradise beyond the touching of hands and seeing of eyes? Shall we see God face to face, walk in the cool of evening, name the animals, count work a joy, see the labor of our hands prosper and know it is good? O, that it might be a place where shame is no more and innocence is never lost. Surely that is Paradise.

Only one knows the mysteries of Paradise, and this one invites thieves to go with him this very day.

This is the day to choose life, to splash in sweet springs, dry in the sun and walk in the footsteps of the one who invites us home.

Paradise is where wholeness fills the heart; rightness falls like dew upon the evening and quenches the thirst of morning. Paradise is where everything comes together, makes sense again, not from the knowledge of argument, but from deep wells of wisdom filled by the soul of the earth.

This is where favorite melodies rock us to rest, and childlike laughter wakens within us each morning.

"Truly I tell you, today you will be with me in Paradise."

The Third Word

"Woman, here is your son." Then he said to the disciple, "
Here is your mother."

John 19:25-27

She hears these words standing on a hill called "Skull." A
place of death. It smells. An aura of suffering hangs heavily
over the cross-pocked landscape. Her son is dying. Hanging
above her, she can hear his labored breathing. Standing at
the foot of his cross, it becomes her cross too as she waits for
him to die.

She is in her forties, a widow, having raised her children
alone since her husband's death. Most Jewish women marry
again if they have no sons, but she has sons and chose to
remain widowed.

This man dying above her is her firstborn. A father figure
for the younger children, he worked in the carpentry shop,
cared for her; a good Jewish boy. They enjoyed many years
as a family in Nazareth before things changed.

One day he walked into their home, sat down next to her on the floor and said he was leaving. She was absolutely shocked, then bewildered. Sons didn't leave home. He was in charge of this family, standing in for Joseph, caring for the household, for her, standing by her sick bed. Some day her deathbed.

Some day he would make her funeral arrangements, finish family business, divide her personal treasures among her children. She assumed he would always be with her as she grew old and lay down to die. She expected him to be with her until the end and manage the details after she took her last breath and returned to the dust from whence Yahweh had given her life.

Suddenly the tables turned. Her son will not wait upon her death. She waits upon his. Life has taken an unnatural twist, a child dying before his mother. She waits for his labored breathing to stop, for blessed silence to signal the end of his suffering.

Within these cruel hours of waiting, she remembers the dreams she once had for her son. Memories of Elizabeth, haunting tunes, magnificent songs of shalom. The hungry fed. The rich sent away empty. Rebellious lyrics not altogether fitting for a girl child.

Cousin Elizabeth's babe was born a few months before she herself labored in Bethlehem. Her son was born to be great, a leader of his people, a servant of Yahweh.

Those long ago angels sang of promises yet to keep. Those kneeling magi now seem but a seductive daydream. John was dead. Now she is watching her own son die. At least Elizabeth didn't have to watch John die.

Where did our boys go wrong? Where did I go wrong? What happened to all the tidings of great joy? And the angels, where did they go?

What was the beginning to this end? Perhaps its genesis rested in breaking the waters of the Jordan as John reluctantly baptized her son. Or was it earlier when her boy loitered about the Temple in Jerusalem asking questions, excusing his behavior to her and Joseph with something about his father's business. What business led him to this end? Not carpentry.

He gasps again for breath. Her head drops. Tears streak her dusty face. Unable to look up at him, she moans and sways and chants, "I held him to my breast and nursed him once, felt his tiny fingers wrap around mine. He smelled so new and clean and sweet.

Now his fingers wrap around nails, and he smells of sweat and death. If he'd stayed in Nazareth in the carpenter's shop, he would have been safe.

He could have studied the Torah and read holy scripture each Sabbath. He might have become a rabbi. I would have been so proud. He could have lived a long, good life, married, given me grandchildren. He should have outlived me."

"Woman, here is your son."

She hears these words and wonders of this man standing near. It doesn't make sense to her, how could it make sense to him? A surrogate son? Surely he wouldn't want the responsibility of an old woman, another old woman, someone else's mother. He has his own life to live, his own relatives to support. You can't pass a mother into the care of another mother's son?

And Mary ponders, "How do I mother a strange man? What does he care for me?

Families are coupled and born, not made with last minute words. Families are bloodlines and birthrights. Relationships are a long time growing, bonded through tribes and traditions, shared joys and sorrows.

This stranger and I have nothing in common, only a cross. We can't come together this late in my life and be family to one another. The only bloodline we share is spilling now upon the ground. Is this sufficient bonding to be family?"

And he says, "Woman, here is your son."

Her heart cries, "Families are born in youth and innocence. Families are born from weddings and parties, not funerals, not crucifixions. How can I start a family over again at the end of my life? How can I birth again in the midst of death? I am too full of tears, too tired to start over.

Yet, you ask us to become a family, a family born of despair. Far from the carefree smiles of my youth, you ask me to conceive of a son in these gray and wrinkled days."

"Woman, here is your son."

Mary ponders these things in her heart, her body aching, weary beyond words. She bends forward, lowering herself to lie upon the ground. Has she ever been so helpless? Labor was hard, but it had an ending. Crucifixion lasts forever, bleeding across the centuries, groaning through history, weeping with timeless grief. She prays he will die quickly.

"How long, O Lord? How long? Hear my cry! Deliver my son.

I'm a shattered family, like pottery dashed upon the path of approaching caravans. I am splintered; my pieces are lost, never again to be whole. This new son I am to behold sees what I see, smells and hears the same death I wait upon. We share no more than whispers and tears."

Neither Mary nor this strange young man is to the other a first choice of family. They share only the agony of one loved by both, and one who loved them both. They are bound by sorrow.

Perhaps with time they may consider the possibility of beginning some new kind of family, some adoptive relationship. It may be that God's family will bond best through the blood, sweat and death of the man who calls.

"Woman, here is your son." Then he said to the disciple, " Here is your mother."

The Fourth Word

"My God! My God! Why have you forsaken me?"

Matthew 27:46

In all creation is there a sadder word than forsaken?

Forsaken is not a choice, not a retreat to quiet garden, no sanctuary sought for contemplation. Forsaken is not an option to leave the busy workplace and discover a moment of repose in pleasant solitude. Forsaken, not a decision to stroll apart from the crowd along the banks of a Galilean sea.

No one chooses forsaken. It is someone else's deliberate act to shun, to disown, to make no eye contact, to pass without breathing a word. It is an abandoned child crying into the darkness, "Daddy, Daddy," straining to hear the father's familiar voice. Then, listening to only the sounds of unbroken silence. This is forsaken.

Forsaken is like the wastes of desert, full of emptiness, no tree or flower, no sounds of life, only long ago echoes of winds whining with no place to blow. Forsaken stretches like an emotional desert blasted by the sands of empty time, dried by famine-colored skies leaving the ground of one's soul cracked and hurting.

Here, one stares through the distance without hope of variation, without a purpose for looking, without a hint of rescue from the awful void of forsaken. Here, the horizon yawns beneath the heavens, flat and aimless with no place to stop and rest.

Can it be the Word of God dies in silence? The Word, who from the beginning was with the Father, is now alone in the hush of his ending. Has it all been a joke, some demonic comedy? Does the Great Creator dangle hope like a carrot and expect this Son of God, this Son of Man to follow God knows where? Does the Great Creator give free will only to manipulate us with empty hope and promises never kept?

Silence feels like the greatest of punishments when longing to hear a voice. A spirit imprisoned in solitary confinement.

This Great Creator of body and soul knows us well, knows our going out and our coming in and the yearnings of our hearts. We are created to feast on hope, on presence, on the daily manna of godly company. This Great Creator of all knowledge knows we can endure almost anything if ABBA be with us, if ABBA be for us, but not if ABBA be silent.

"Why have you forsaken me?" Five words, unanswered, heartbreaking, left hanging in the silence of fetid afternoon air. An agonizing question drenched with body odor and fresh blood.

There was a time this dying man had yearned to be alone, away from the demands of the crowds, away from the pushing and shoving of hands and elbows, the pushing and shoving of questions and demands, the pushing and shoving of institutional religion. There was a time not so very long ago, this man would have been grateful for solitude.

There had never been enough time to think and sort out his questions in those days. Never enough time to evaluate the path he had walked these last three years. He tried to find time on the water, to pray and read and think about another kingdom, another ruler, and another rule.

Time was, this man being crucified struggled to get away from the multitudes to be alone with God. He never dreamed he might someday be forsaken.

From a distance they watch him suffering with his question still unanswered, dying to know why this is happening, this way, now. Leaning forward with anticipation, some wait for his last-minute rescue. A just-in-the-nick-of-time deliverance.

Perhaps another dove will descend, liberating the son in whom God is well pleased. Possibly a heavenly host will swoop down upon Golgotha to rescue the dying one.

Jesus might be lifted gently from the cross, ministered unto by angels, wounds rubbed with healing balm and swaddled with linen cloths. He might then recover in the loving care of those who had known his own healing touch. They could return his favors. But the healer remains wounded, dying and forsaken.

Hearts ache, straining for this final act to end. But nothing happens, nothing at all, only God's silence.

Uncomfortable with silence, those who wait upon his death listen for inspirational words. Might Jesus have a final statement, something to repeat through the ages, something to demonstrate his spiritual strength, to proclaim his faith in spite of God's silence. Perhaps there is a manifesto upon his lips, a testimony to reverberate throughout history, or a blessing for the dying to offer at every deathbed, every funeral, every grave. No, only dead air.

And, "My God! My God! Why have you forsaken me?"

Those who stand beneath his cross see only an ordinary man dying, suffering beyond imagination and utterly forsaken.

Those who wait can't help but wonder, "How shall I die?" It's not so much the fear of death as the fear of dying. Those who witness death know the fragility of life, the reality of terminal existence. In the wee small hours of the morning, each wonders, "Shall I linger or go in the twinkling of an eye? Shall I have time to put my business in order, plan my memorial service, tell my loved ones good-bye?"

Those who wait find no prescription for dying. The man on the cross utters no special words of benediction for the crowds to remember, no comforting formula to speak at a bed of death, or to console as breath departs for the final time.

Those who wait wonder how their end will be. Each will have questions, perhaps the same question, "My God, my God, why have you forsaken me?" and feel the emptiness of silence. Each knows death will not be denied its day. There is no rescue from this end. All will die. But, die alone?

Someday, we too shall die as Jesus dies. We are human, crying at birth, crying at death. Like Jesus, we too live questioning the meaning of life, the meaning of death, the meaning of the in-between.

Because Jesus dies knowing how it feels to be forsaken, how it feels to die with a question hanging between life and death, because Jesus knows excruciating silence, we need not fear our end. Jesus will not forsake us.

Our God, who is the Word, does not always speak. Our God, who is the Word, may choose silence to communicate in the pause of suffering, may choose absolute quiet to comfort in the hush of tenebrous shadows, may choose to breathe stillness upon us at the end.

Our God, who is the Crucified One, the first forsaken for our sakes, from him the fullness of silence we learn. From this God, our horizon of desert wastes is now broken by the vertical relief of a cross.   From this God, the first seeds of eternal life are planted in the cracks of our brokenness, and from the tears of this Crucified One the seeds are watered and grow.

For our sakes, Christ is forsaken.

"My God, my God, why have you forsaken me?"

The Fifth Word

"I am thirsty."

John 19:28

Can it be the Living Water thirsts? This Son of God, came to water our dry lives, bring us living water. How then can the Living Water thirst?

Parched lips cry for water to quench a dying thirst. Thirsty like the desert wasteland awaiting spring rains. Parched like the dusty plains holding their breaths, listening for thunder, hushed and waiting. There is no mountain spring bubbling fresh and clear for the Living Water. The fount is dry. The earth is baked. It cracks, breaks open.

Once, in the land of Cana of Galilee, water changed to fine wine for a wedding feast. His mother came to him and said, "What will you do, the wine has run out?" And he responded, "Woman, what concern is that to you and to me? My hour has not yet come."

But she continued as though she had not heard, and turning to the servants said, "Do whatever he tells you."

Standing near at hand were six, stone jars for the Jewish rites of purification. "Fill the jars with water," he said. And when they were filled to the brim, the servants drew some out and took it to the chief steward. It was the finest of wine. From where did it come?

Every host serves the best wine first and when the tongue is dulled, the inferior is poured for guests. Not so here. Old jars for waters of purification poured forth a vintage delight. Might another miracle pour forth upon this Living Water as he hangs upon his cross?

And Jesus says, "I am thirsty."

This one who walks upon the water and calms the storm, this one thirsts. His hand it was that stilled the waves and calmed the sea. His hand reached out to Peter, beckoning him to come across the waves. His hands pulled nets from the waters filled with the catch of the day. His hands pointed to dry land, calling his friends to leave the water and fish for men. This man thirsts. The fountain of living waters is dry.

Crying for water is the same man who tied a towel around his waist, filled a bowl and knelt to splash water upon the feet of his friends.

They had gathered for supper, climbed the stairs to an upper room and waited for a servant to wash their feet. No one came.

Jesus took this lowly role.

He bowed to lift each calloused foot, washed the dust from these weary men, cleansed the cuts from rocks and weeds along the way, and rubbed into each the sweet lavender of nard. So cooling. So soothing. He gave them water, and more.

Now dying, he is denied water.

O God, you who created the water and dry land, be gracious unto him. Give him to drink. You, who parted the Red Sea, deliver your son. You, who caused the seas to swarm with living creatures, give him to drink. He is thirsty.

When the Israelites cried out for water in the wilderness, it was you, O Lord, who stood before Moses at Horeb, you who commanded him to strike the rock, you who caused the rock to gush forth water and give drink to your people. Even their livestock drank from your handiwork.

Why not your son? Why bring him out of Egypt only to let him die thirsting in this wretched place, a land strewn with dry bones, dry souls, and dried up dreams tossing in the wind. The lands thirst; the hills parch waiting with springtime anticipation. The whole world is drying up with the thirst of this man.

Setting his face like flint, striking out for Jerusalem, entering the very place infamous for short-lived prophets, now he hangs thirsting outside that city's walls.

Long ago this thirsty man was born in the breaking of his mother's waters. He suckled at her breast, drinking with the sounds of baby thirst. He ran the hills of Galilee kicking up rocks and sand, knowing he could dash home to drink from a deep well of cool water. Coming up out of the Jordan, brushing wet hair from his eyes, he heard you speak his name, calling him Beloved. Now, O Lord, your Beloved thirsts, dying in the spilling of blood and water from his side. Thirsty.

Does our life really pass before us as we die?

If so, he remembers the desert, the wilderness of his temptation. His ministry began in dry wastelands, began with temptation. It was from the waters of baptism Jesus was led by the Spirit into the desert wilds, where for forty days he was tempted by demonic company. Hunger growled in the depths of his being, and the evil one taunted, "If you are the Son of God, command this stone to become a loaf of bread." But Jesus knew he did not live by bread alone.

Worldly power was offered him if he would worship the tempter. But Jesus knew worship belonged to the Lord God. Why not test God's protection by jumping from the pinnacle of the temple? Let the angels bear him up so not even his foot will dash upon the stones. But Jesus would not put God to the test.

On the cross the Living Water is tempted again. Soldiers call to him from below, "If you are the Savior, save yourself." Tragic human irony, his life ending with temptation as it began. But this time the Evil One is silent. With so many others to play his role and speak his words, there is no need to waste his voice.

Let the soldiers heckle him. Let the passers by call out cruel insults. So Evil waits, lurking through the crowd, smelling the sweat of cruelty, hearing the taunts of stupidity, licking up the rains of showering curses. Evil drinks deeply while the Son of God thirsts.

"I am thirsty," he calls.

Vinegar for the one who turned water to the finest wine. Vinegar for him who calmed the sea, and reached his hand to Peter. Cruelty answers a last request for water. Sour wine on a sponge, the last taste on his lips. This man who created the best wedding wine for last is given vinegar at his last, and his ending leaves the world with sour grapes setting teeth on edge from generation to generation.

And they taunted, "If you are the King of the Jews, save yourself."

O, God, you who cause the desert to bloom after spring rains, your son thirsts. O, Alpha and Omega, the first and the last, you who to the thirsty give water as a gift from the spring of life, answer his request. O, Abba Father, you who did not let the cup pass from your son's lips as he prayed in the garden, fill a cup with water. Hold it to his lips. Your son calls,

"I am thirsty."

The Sixth Word

"It is finished."

John 19:30

Is it ever finished?

Life ends, but is the purpose of life finished with death? Most people die feeling unfinished, having left many things undone, unsaid, unfulfilled.   Trusting others to complete a manuscript, a song, a drawing, a message, a destiny. But, is it ever possible to finish the work of another?

Had this man on the cross lived a full life and died at a rich old age, would we have known more about the Kingdom and his Abba in heaven? Three years is such a short time to complete the work of a lifetime. Three years is hardly getting started, hardly forming one's argument for any kind of change in the world. We must wonder. Is the work of Jesus complete, his mission fulfilled, is there nothing more he could have done?

These thoughts must hang with him upon the cross.   The Kingdom of God is far from being realized. The poor are still poor; the rich are still high and mighty, lifted up above the squalor of the streets, protected by gated communities. Justice is still a dream. Peace a whisper. The Kingdom is not come.

Where have all the promises gone?

He remembers stories his mother told him, stories of angels and magi, of Simeon and Anna. A narrow escape to Egypt and back, just ahead of the baby killers. Echoes of "Great joy to all peoples," remain only echoes. Who is really happy? Where is the joy? Oh, the soldiers are laughing, the crowds jeering, and religious officials look smug. But this is not joy.

"Peace on earth." There is no peace, only the absence of war. No peace, only silence among those too hungry to raise their voices or do violence. No peace, only the hush of terror here on this hill of the skull.

"Good will toward all people. "

Suspicion and fear and division slink among the crowd. People divided, nations divided, religion divided. Bad will toward all people hangs heavy upon the earth, like a curtain fallen too soon at an unfinished play, and no one claps. The story line is suspended between God's tragedy and the devil's comedy.

It is finished, but not over. There are still promises to keep.

Yahweh promised a savior who would tumble princes from their thrones, a savior to exalt the lowly, but the powers of this world are crucifying a simple carpenter, an itinerant preacher, a man who did no harm. Exalted? Yes, lifted upon a cross.

Yahweh promised the hungry would be filled with good things and the rich sent away empty. The hungry still die with bloated bellies. The rich still live with bulging pockets. You can't eat promises, especially unfinished promises.

Life ends too soon. There is always one more spring to smell, one more grandchild to see born, married, settled. One more kiss. One more time to make love. Life ends too soon. Much too soon.

We would see again the work of our hands flourish, live in the homes we build, drink fine wine from the vines we plant, feel the shade of trees we pruned, and harvest their fruits.

Life is never long enough. That twinkling of an eye we are given to live is never enough. Our appetite for life is only whetted.

God's Kingdom is the whisper of an almost remembered dream, half finished when the dawn nudges us awake. It is a refrain following us through the day, a quick glimpse here, a flash of memory there, a promise to tease and flirt with the reality of unfinished business in the streets of our daily life. The work is not finished. A life is ending, but leaving more to do.

Those who look on from afar, wonder, "Is this all there is?"

They believed this man to be sent by God. He would fulfill the promise of a messiah, change the power structure, bring a just society.

Riding into Jerusalem, he had the crowd in his hands. Waving palms and laying their cloaks upon the ground, they welcomed him into the city. Such enthusiasm! He could have rallied the crowd, and caused an insurrection. But he didn't.

They would have followed him. They had followed lesser men. Poor ones have little to lose. Well, their lives, yes, but their lives are not worth living most of the time. Why not gamble a life for a cause? This present life can't get much worse. Why not risk following this man? He seems trustworthy, wants nothing for himself, gives and gives until he is exhausted. And now, he doesn't light the sparks of rebellion to ignite the crowd. He rides on.

On to the Temple.

Those who traffic in religious commerce had a surprise coming. Things were going according to the Passover routine until a mad man pushed his way through the moneychangers and sellers of sacrifice. Tables turned over! Shouts! Money rolled beneath the feet of people who knew not what to do, run from him or collect the coins.

Doves set free, flapped the air with eager freedom. Larger animals joined in the fearful sounds of alarm. Some ran wild, pushing to the ground the weak and old.

Few saw the cause of such a commotion; just felt the wave of its effect. Some noticed an angry man. He alone could explain his actions. He alone could explain his fury. He alone could see the insidious depth of thievery in the temple. Anger abated, he slipped off into the crowd.

Finished?   Not yet. This man ate the Passover, broke the bread, lifted the cup. He sang with his friends and left. This man retreated to the Gethsemane garden to pray for the passing of a final cup. Those closest to him waited, and fell asleep smelling of wine.

Hell broke loose into confusion. There was a kiss and Jesus was taken. Trials. Accusations. Denials. He passed from court to court, beaten, sentenced, thorn crowned. He dragged his own cross to a hill outside the city. With the pounding of nails, he screamed.

As he hangs dying, darkness comes upon the earth at an untimely hour. While shrouded in the mystery of noonday shade, an earthquake obeys his voice and the curtain of the temple is torn in two.

With every breath, there is agony. Those who recognize the signs of death know it is soon over. And soon...

"It is finished."

The Seventh Word

"Father, into your hands I commend my spirit."

Luke 23:46

Life is lived not in days or months or years, but in moments.

Life is made of fragments, bits and pieces of memory stitched together, careless of timely order, arranged by feelings, smells, tastes and touch. The sight of a beloved, the chords of a requiem, these are precious remnants testifying to a life.

The end is soon.

Long ago, in the beginning, God's hands touched earth as a gardener, making good each new thing. The light and dark, the waters and dry lands, every crawling and swimming and flying creature knew the touch of this Creator.

Then it was, in the timeliness of our beginning, heavenly hands gathered dust, fashioned a human body and blew life into it's nostrils.   This handmade image of God felt the earth's goodness, romped with the beasts, smiled with the dawn and felt lonely at sunset.

So it was a soul mate was formed of bone and flesh. Nakedness was celebrated. God looked upon creation and it was very good.

Why couldn't it last?

Disobedience was born within this genesis union. Knowledge is stolen. Shame clothed the goodness of innocence. God's hands fashioned garments of skin for the man and woman, clothing them for their sojourn east of Eden, sending them forth out of the garden. Disciplined but not destroyed.

And so it was history began, stories of trial and error, goodness and evil, birth and death, all touched by the hands of God.

These hands of the Almighty led desert nomads, poured rain to cover the earth, cut rainbows across the skies, tumbled towers built to reach heaven, touched an old man and woman with new life and a nation of descendants numbered like the stars in the sky.

These same hands plagued kings, rescued slaves, rolled back a red sea, spread manna each morning and poured water from dry cracks in desert rocks. God's hands cut rock with commandments, then tossed thunder and unleashed lightning upon the people who grew tired of waiting upon Moses.

For long years, God's hands touched the lips of prophets, anointed kings, filled cups to overflowing, smote enemies, walked with the chosen into captivity, gathered lost lambs and carried them home. Over and over again, these hands rescued the strays, until...

In Bethlehem, God's hands prepared fresh straw for a birthing bed. Reaching low into a stable, calming as the stroke of a midwife cooling a mother's brow, wiping away afterbirth and wrapping swaddling cloths around a bundle of birth cries.

The Word of God in the hands of God, crying his first words.

God's hands were felt in the touch of a mother, lifting a child to her breast. God's hands were felt through those of Joseph, guiding a young boy's bruised fingers as he hammered and sawed. God's hands touched children as Jesus lifted them onto his lap, as he broke the loaves and shared the fish, as he touched the blind, the lepers, the women.

Through Jesus, God's hands touched the earth with healing.

Now it is, with his own bleeding hands curled around nails, Jesus calls for the touch of his father, for Abba's hands to lift his spirit from the cross. He calls for rescue to a place where his spirit will find laugher again, a place to run with the breath of a child, a place to sing alleluias each morning.

The Word of God in the hands of God, crying his last words.

" Father, into your hands I commend my spirit."

And of spirit, what shall we say? God's breath captured in clay. A spark igniting dry bones. Perhaps the gardener's dust fashioned for the planting of eternity.

Spirit, that image bonding us to the source of our reflection. Spirit, that which abides as welcome guest in our earthly temple. Spirit, that unique quality which stamps us like no other and casts the likeness of our mantel upon those who pass our way. Spirit, an eternal whisper beyond our finest imagining, shared by God with creative humility, sustained in spite of our earth-bound understanding.

Yet, the spirit of God is not bound by things of this earth. At the Jordan, God's spirit descended like a dove and traveled with the Beloved, allowing him to baptize others with God's blessing.

Blessings overflowed to the poor in spirit, the meek, the merciful and those who mourned. And to the peacemakers, the pure in heart and the persecuted, the Beloved offered kinship in the Kingdom. He saw in them the likeness of God, the spirit of light and salt, of sharing and hospitality. Words of God are spoken by the Beloved Word. The gifts of God for the people of God, through the hands of the Beloved.

"Father, into thy hands I commend my spirit."

Only God's hands can hold a spirit. And so it is, Jesus gives his spirit into the hands of his Father, returning from whence it came. Only the hands of God can hold the unseen, the future, the potential, the unfinished, that which is yet to be born.

Entrusted to the one who is the Alpha and the Omega, we know the good work of our hands will be made complete. Carried by the Good Shepherd, we will be home by the end of the day. That which is formless, having left the host, will be cupped in the palm of God's hands. Weary and heavy laden, Jesus' spirit will be gathered into the everlasting arms, untroubled by the past, comforted by the familiar and revived by the breath of God. His spirit will be home.

God's home is where there are no limitations, no betrayal, no pain. Here, no dark glass to see through dimly. Here, God's first born will inherit his birthright. Here he sees face to face. He is home.

"Father, into your hands I commend my spirit."

About the Author

Sylvia Casberg attended San Francisco Theological Seminary as a second career student. She received her Master of Divinity and Doctor of Ministry degrees there in 1982 and 1989.

After serving Wellshire Presbyterian Church, in Denver, CO, she became Chaplain of the Moscow Protestant Chaplaincy in Moscow, Russia.

In 1998, Sylvia traveled the Middle East to research a book for the Presbyterian Church, (USA) and to photograph the projects of the Jinishian Memorial Program. "Serving the Least of These" was published in 2000.

Returning to the States, Sylvia was called as a chaplain to the University of Colorado Hospital shortly before 9/11.

She has served the Presbyterian Church (USA) in peacemaking, social justice and mission.

The birth of Sylvia's grandson brought her to California in 2005. Here she was installed as Associate Pastor of Bethania Lutheran Church, in Solvang.

Retiring in 2009, Sylvia is writing and publishing full time, except when she's being a grandmother.

www.SunnyFieldsPublishing.com

www.ingramcontent.com/pod-product-compliance
Lightning Source LLC
Chambersburg PA
CBHW021224020426
42331CB00003B/459